SESMA
Children's
Bilingual
PICTURE
DICTIONARY

English - Portuguese

Inglês - Português

Illustrations by J. Quezada
Published by Bilingual Dictionaries, Inc.

Bilingual Dictionaries, Inc.

SESMA Children's Bilingual Picture Dictionary
English-Portuguese Edition
2nd Edition

Illustrations & Cover
Jose Quezada

Content & Design
Alex Sesma
Jose Quezada

Editor
C. Sesma, M.A.
Alex Sesma

Translation
Ana Rita Craveiro

Publisher
Bilingual Dictionaries, Inc.

Copyright © 2019 by Bilingual Dictionaries, Inc.
All rights reserved. No part of this book may be reproduced, transmitted, stored, or used in any form or by any means graphic, electronic, or mechanical, including but not limited to photocopying, recording, scanning, digitizing, taping, information storage, database or retrieval system, or online distribution, except as permitted under the United States Copyright Act of 1976, without the prior written permission of the publisher.

Bilingual Dictionaries, Inc.
PO Box 1154, Murrieta, CA 92564, USA
Email: support@bilingualdictionaries.com

ISBN13: 978-0-933146-05-1

For information about the SESMA Picture Dictionary series and other bilingual educational materials visit:
www.BilingualDictionaries.com

SESMA Picture Dictionary

More than 1000 Illustrations

A simple bilingual picture dictionary with fun illustrations. Great for children ages 5-12.

Mais de 1000 Ilustrações

Um dicionário simples de imagens bilingue com ilustrações divertidas. Ótimo para crianças em idades 5-12.

Lots of Languages

We are proud to publish the SESMA Picture Dictionary in many different languages from around the world. Find all our language editions online.

Muitos idiomas

Temos orgulho de publicar o Dicionário de Imagens SESMA em muitos idiomas diferentes de todo o mundo. Encontre todas as nossas edições de idiomas online.

Hello Привет こんにちは *Ciao* **Bonjour** ولی و *Sawubona* 여보세요 *Hola* 你好 **Hallo** Olá

BilingualDictionaries.com

Buy Now

The new and improved SESMA Picture Dictionary is back! Purchase bilingual educational materials in over 50 languages.

Compre agora

O novo e melhorado Dicionário de Imagens SESMA está de volta! Compre materiais educacionais bilingues em mais de 50 idiomas.

Table of Contents

Table of Contents

Numbers

0	**1**	**2**	**3**
zero zero	**one** um	**two** dois	**three** três

4	**5**	**6**	**7**
four quatro	**five** cinco	**six** seis	**seven** sete

8	**9**	**10**	**11**
eight oito	**nine** nove	**ten** dez	**eleven** onze

12	**13**	**14**	**15**
twelve doze	**thirteen** treze	**fourteen** catorze	**fifteen** quinze

16	**17**	**18**	**19**
sixteen dezasseis	**seventeen** dezassete	**eighteen** dezoito	**nineteen** dezanove

20	**30**	**40**	**50**
twenty vinte	**thirty** trinta	**forty** quarenta	**fifty** cinquenta

60	**70**	**80**	**90**
sixty sessenta	**seventy** setenta	**eighty** oitenta	**ninety** noventa

Números

Numbers

100
one hundred
cem

1,000
one thousand
mil

1,000,000
one million
um milhão

1,000,000,000
one billion
um bilião

1st
first
primeiro

2nd
second
segundo

3rd
third
terceiro

4th
fourth
quarto

5th
fifth
quinto

6th
sixth
sexto

7th
seventh
sétimo

8th
eighth
oitavo

9th
ninth
nono

10th
tenth
décimo

11th
eleventh
décimo primeiro

12th
twelfth
décimo segundo

13th
thirteenth
décimo terceiro

14th
fourteenth
décimo quarto

15th
fifteenth
décimo quinto

16th
sixteenth
décimo sexto

17th
seventeenth
décimo sétimo

18th
eighteenth
décimo oitavo

19th
nineteenth
décimo nono

20th
twentieth
vigésimo

Colors

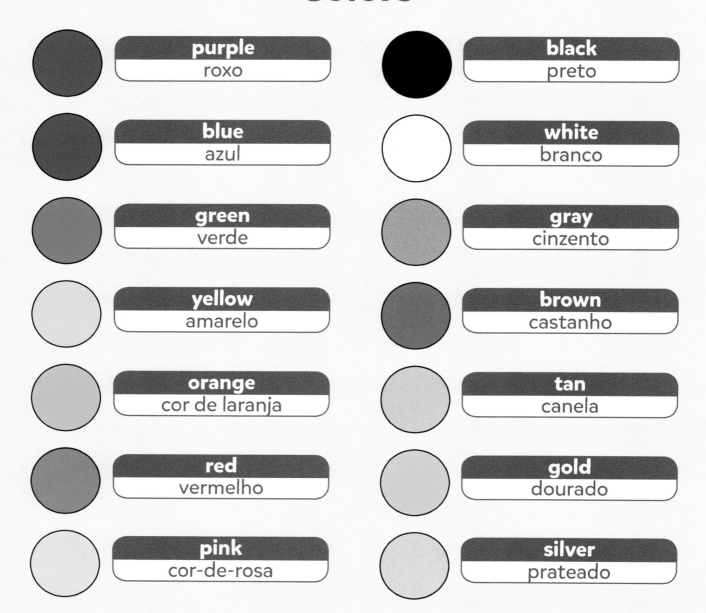

purple / roxo	**black** / preto
blue / azul	**white** / branco
green / verde	**gray** / cinzento
yellow / amarelo	**brown** / castanho
orange / cor de laranja	**tan** / canela
red / vermelho	**gold** / dourado
pink / cor-de-rosa	**silver** / prateado

Cores

Shapes

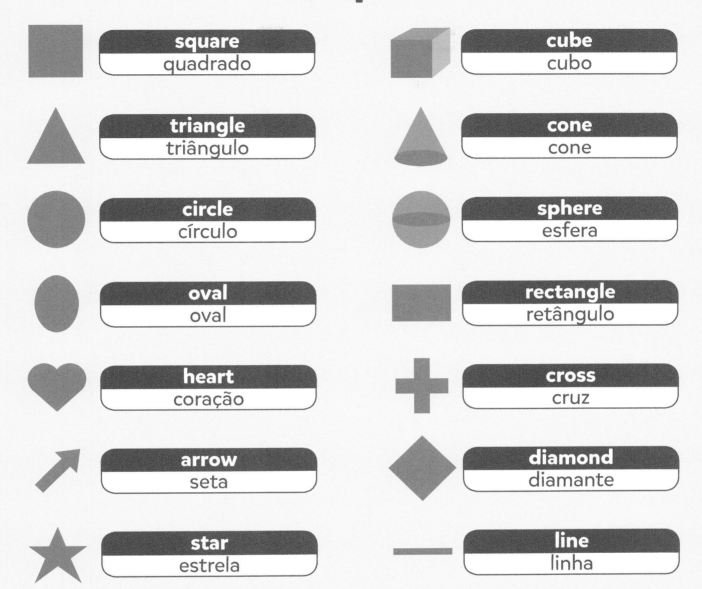

■	**square** / quadrado	▪ cube	**cube** / cubo
▲	**triangle** / triângulo	▲	**cone** / cone
●	**circle** / círculo	●	**sphere** / esfera
●	**oval** / oval	▪	**rectangle** / retângulo
♥	**heart** / coração	✚	**cross** / cruz
➚	**arrow** / seta	◆	**diamond** / diamante
★	**star** / estrela	—	**line** / linha

Calendar

calendar
calendário

12/31/1999

date
data

month
mês

day
dia

year
ano

January
janeiro

February
fevereiro

March
março

April
abril

May
maio

June
junho

July
julho

August
agosto

September
setembro

October
outubro

November
novembro

December
dezembro

Calendário

Calendar

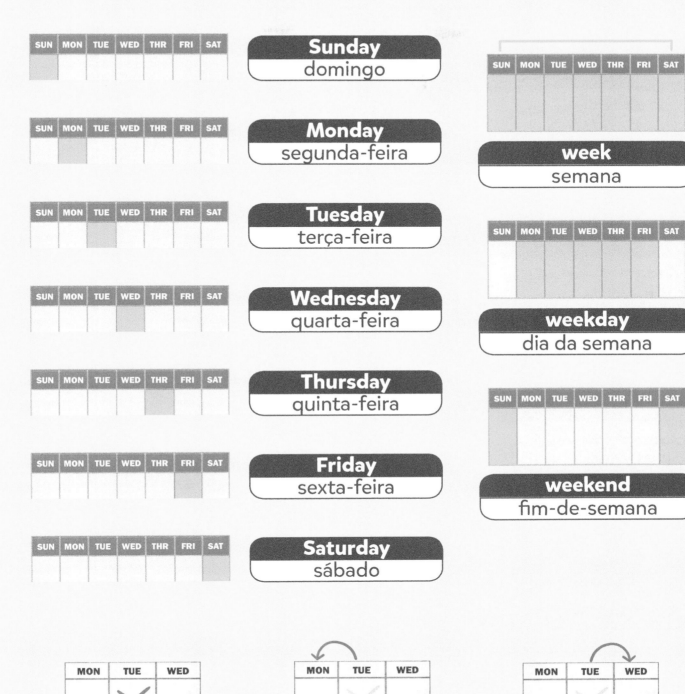

SUN	MON	TUE	WED	THR	FRI	SAT

Sunday
domingo

Monday
segunda-feira

Tuesday
terça-feira

Wednesday
quarta-feira

Thursday
quinta-feira

Friday
sexta-feira

Saturday
sábado

week
semana

weekday
dia da semana

weekend
fim-de-semana

today
hoje

yesterday
ontem

tomorrow
amanhã

Greetings

hello
olá

goodbye
adeus

please
por favor

thank you
obrigado

yes
sim

no
não

Questions ?

who
quem

what
o que

when
quando

where
onde

why
porquê

how
como

Perguntas ?

When?

time
tempo

twelve o' clock
doze horas

one o' clock
uma hora

two o'clock
duas horas

three o'clock
três horas

four o'clock
quatro horas

five o'clock
cinco horas

six o'clock
seis horas

seven o'clock
sete horas

eight o'clock
oito horas

nine o'clock
nove horas

ten o'clock
dez horas

eleven o'clock
onze horas

Quando?

When?

sunrise
nascer do sol

noon
meio dia

sunset
pôr do sol

midnight
meia noite

one fifteen
uma e quinze

quarter past one
uma e um quarto

one thirty
uma e trinta

half past one
uma e meia

one forty-five
uma e quarenta e cinco

a quarter to two
um quarto para as duas

hour
hora

minute
minuto

second
segundo

Quando?

Where?

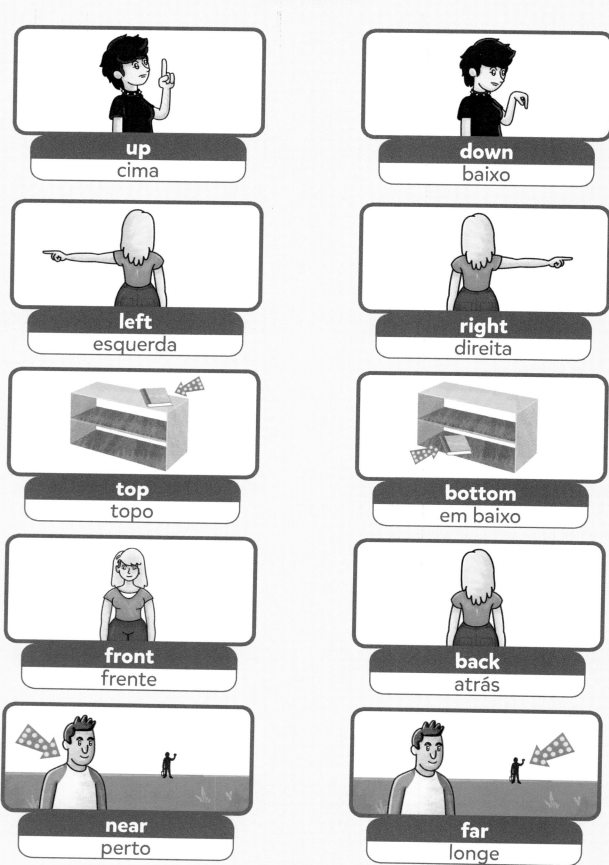

up
cima

down
baixo

left
esquerda

right
direita

top
topo

bottom
em baixo

front
frente

back
atrás

near
perto

far
longe

Onde?

Where?

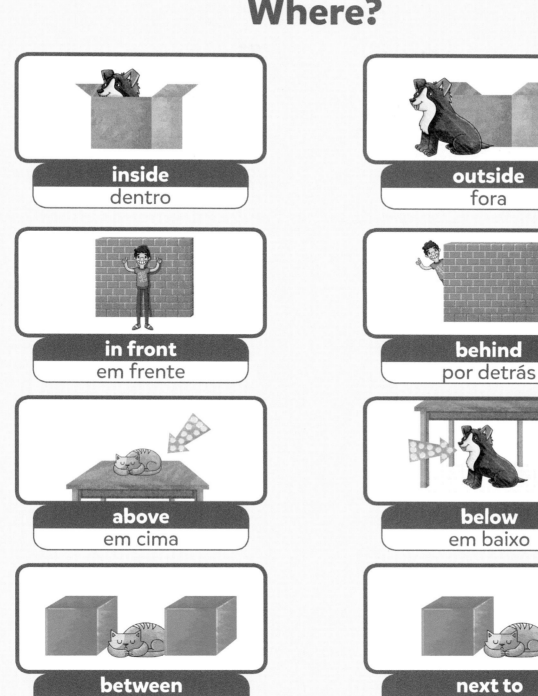

inside
dentro

outside
fora

in front
em frente

behind
por detrás

above
em cima

below
em baixo

between
entre

next to
ao lado de

over
sobre

under
debaixo

Onde?

17

Money (USA)

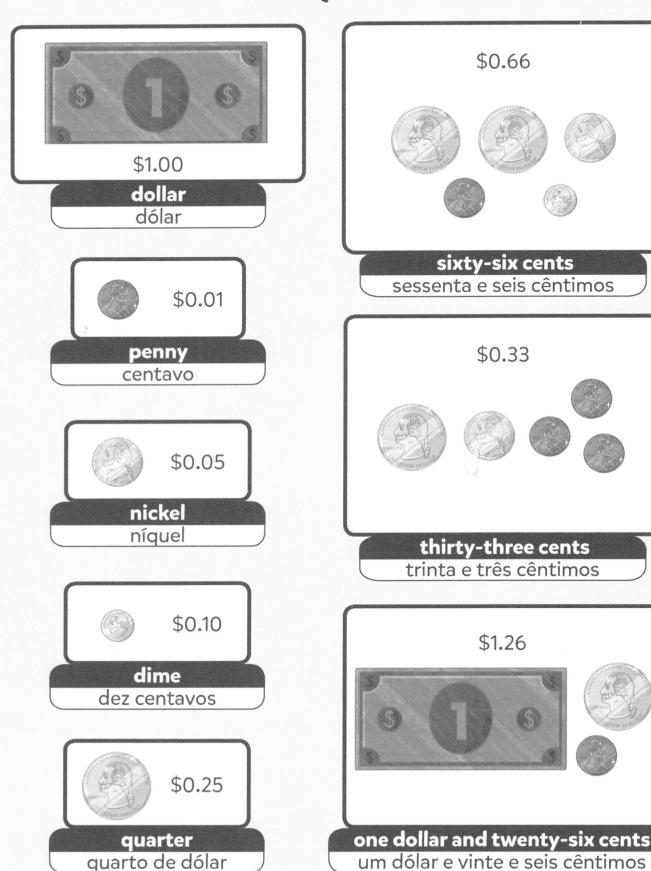

$1.00
dollar
dólar

$0.01
penny
centavo

$0.05
nickel
níquel

$0.10
dime
dez centavos

$0.25
quarter
quarto de dólar

$0.66
sixty-six cents
sessenta e seis cêntimos

$0.33
thirty-three cents
trinta e três cêntimos

$1.26
one dollar and twenty-six cents
um dólar e vinte e seis cêntimos

Dinheiro

Chapter 1
Family

Capítulo 1
Família

Family

1. grandmother

2. grandfather

3. aunt

4. mother

5. father

6. uncle

7. brother

8. sister

9. cousin

1. avó	2. avô	3. tia
4. mãe	5. pai	6. tio
7. irmão	8. irmã	9. primo

Família

Family

1. parents

2. children

3. husband and wife

4. son and daughter

1. pais

2. filhos

3. marido e mulher

4. filho e filha

5. sobrinha e sobrinho

5. niece and nephew

Family • Age

1. baby

2. child

3. teenager

4. adult

5. senior

6. woman

7. girl

8. boy

9. man

1. bebé

2. criança

3. adolescente

4. adulto

5. sénior

6. mulher

7. rapariga

8. rapaz

9. homem

Família • Idade

Family • Description

1. handsome

2. pretty

3. ugly

4. skinny

5. tall

6. young

7. fat

8. short

9. old

1. giro	2. bonito	3. feio
4. magro	5. alto	6. novo
7. gordo	8. baixo	9. velho

Family • Birthday

1. birthday

2. cake

3. candle

4. balloon

5. gift

6. party

7. friend

8. game

9. fun

1. aniversário	2. bolo	3. vela
4. balão	5. prenda	6. festa
7. amigo	8. jogo	9. divertido

Family · Wedding

1. wedding

2. bride

3. groom

4. to cry

5. to dance

6. to laugh

7. to love

8. to kiss

9. to hug

1. casamento	2. noiva	3. noivo
4. chorar	5. dançar	6. rir
7. amar	8. beijar	9. abraçar

Família · Casamento

Family • Emotions

1. happy

2. sad

3. scared

4. angry

5. surprised

6. excited

7. embarrassed

8. proud

9. shy

1. feliz	2. triste	3. assustado
4. zangado	5. surpreso	6. excitado
7. embaraçado	8. orgulhoso	9. tímido

Chapter 2
Home

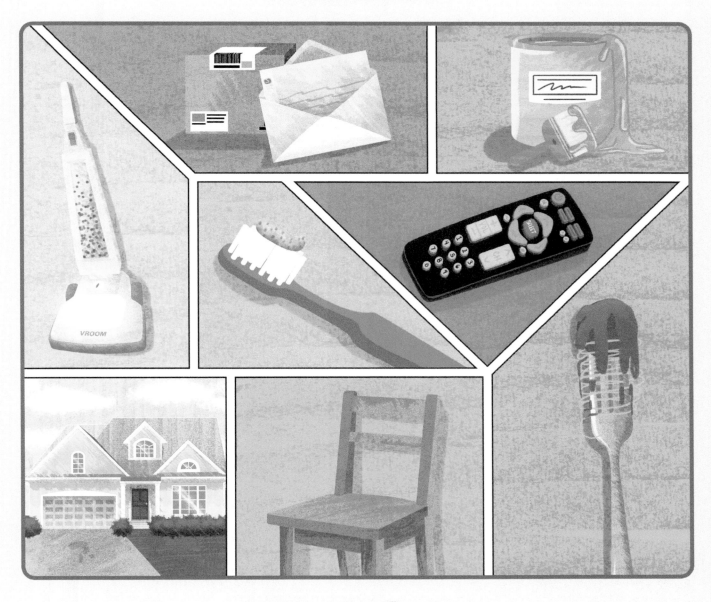

Capítulo 2
Casa

Home

1.house

2.apartment

3.door

4.window

5.doorknob

6.doorbell

7.key

8.to knock

9.to ring
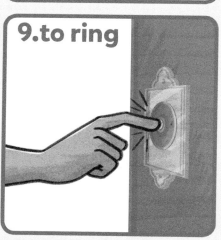

1.casa	2.apartamento	3.porta
4.janela	5.maçaneta	6.campainha
7.chave	8.bater	9.tocar

Home

1.stairs
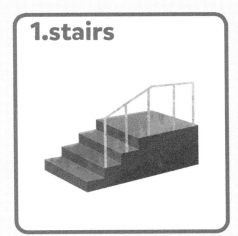

2.roof

3.chimney

4.gate
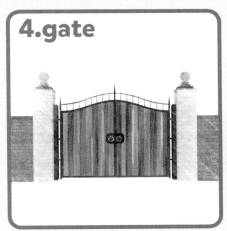

5.garage

6.fence

7.mailbox

8.mail

9.to receive

1.escadas	2.telhado	3.chaminé
4.portão	5.garagem	6.cerca
7.caixa do correio	8.correio	9.receber

Home

1. kitchen

2. bedroom

3. bathroom

4. living room

5. yard

1. cozinha

2. quarto

3. casa de banho

4. sala de estar

5. jardim

Casa

Home

1. neighbor

2. to meet

3. to invite

4. to wave

1. vizinho

2. conhecer

3. convidar

4. acenar

5. brincar

5. to play

Home • Kitchen

1.refrigerator

2.dishwasher

3.microwave

4.toaster

5.stove

6.oven

7.sink

8.counter

9.cupboard

1.frigorífico	2.lava-louças	3.micro-ondas
4.torradeira	5.fogão	6.forno
7.lava loiças	8.bancada	9.armário

Home · Kitchen

1.plate

2.bowl

3.cup

4.knife

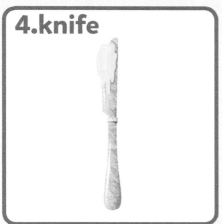

5.fork

6.spoon

7.table

8.chair

9.napkin

1.prato	2.taça	3.copo
4.faca	5.garfo	6.colher
7.mesa	8.cadeira	9.guardanapo

Casa · Cozinha

Home • Bedroom

1.bed

2.pillow

3.blanket

4.dresser

5.nightstand

6.lamp

7.closet

8.poster
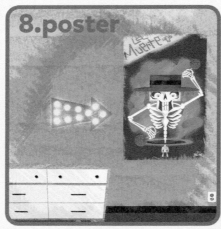

9.light

1.cama	2.almofada	3.cobertor
4.cómoda	5.mesa de cabeceira	6.candeeiro
7.armário da roupa	8.poster	9.luz

Home • Bedroom

1. dream

2. nightmare

3. tired

4. awake

1. sonho

2. pesadelo

3. cansado

4. acordado

5. dormir

5. to sleep

Home • Bathroom

1.shower 	**2.bathtub** 	**3.faucet** 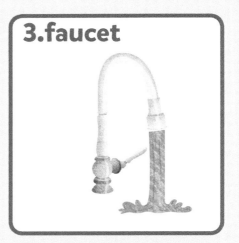
4.mirror 	**5.toilet** 	**6.toilet paper** 
7.hamper 	**8.comb** 	**9.soap** 

1.chuveiro	2.banheira	3.torneira
4.espelho	5.sanita	6.papel higiénico
7.cesto de roupas	8.pente	9.sabonete

Home • Bathroom

1.toothbrush 	**2.toothpaste** 	**3.towel** 
4.floss 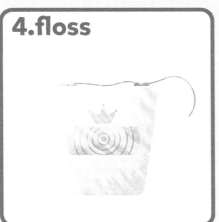	**5.wet** 	**6.dry** 
7.lotion 	**8.clean** 	**9.dirty** 

1.escova de dentes	2.pasta de dentes	3.toalha
4.fio dental	5.molhado	6.seco
7.loção	8.limpo	9.sujo

Home • Bathroom

1. to open

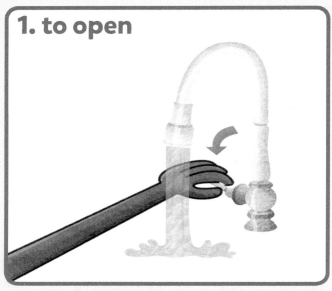

2. to close

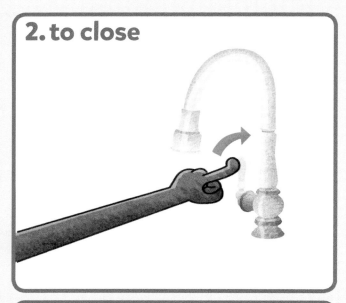

3. to comb

4. to brush

5. to shower

1. abrir

2. fechar

3. pentear

4. escovar

5. tomar banho

Casa • Banheiro

Home • Living Room

1.wall

2.floor

3.ceiling

4.couch

5.carpet

6.outlet

7.fireplace

8.painting

9.switch

1.parede	2.chão	3.teto
4.sofá	5.carpete	6.tomada
7.lareira	8.quadro	9.interruptor

Casa • Sala de estar

Home • Living Room

1.television

2.tablet

3.screen

4.remote

5.video game

6.board game

7.toy

8.off

9.on
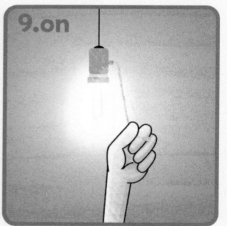

1.televisão	2.tablet	3.ecrã
4.comando	5.video jogo	6.jogo de tabuleiro
7.brinquedo	8.desligado	9.ligado

Home • Living Room

1. together

2. alone

3. to watch

4. to cheer

WOOOOOO

1. juntos

2. sozinho

3. assistir

4. animar

5. confortável

5. comfortable

Home • Yard

1.lawn	2.garden	3.barbecue

4.lawn mower	5.trash	6.hose

7.dog house	8.tree house	9.sprinkler

1.relvado	2.jardim, horta	3.churrasco
4.cortador de relva	5.lixo	6.mangueira
7.casota	8.casa da árvore	9.aspersor

Home • Garage

1.paint

2.ladder

3.cooler

4.fan

5.box

6.bag

7.to lift

8.to carry

9.to fall

1.tinta	2.escadote	3.geladeira
4.ventoinha	5.caixa	6.saco
7.levantar	8.carregar	9.cair

Home · Tool

1.hammer

2.nail

3.screwdriver
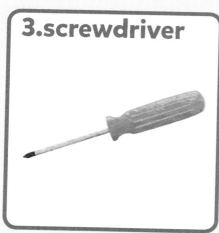

4.power drill

5.toolbox

6.wrench

7.tape

8.to break

9.to fix

1.martelo	2.prego	3.chave de fendas
4.berbequim	5.caixa de ferramentas	6.chave inglesa
7.fita cola	8.partir	9.arranjar

Home • Clean

1.broom

2.dustpan

3.mop
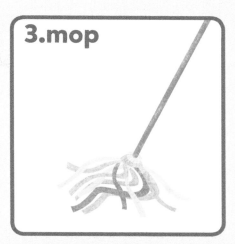

4.sponge

5.vacuum
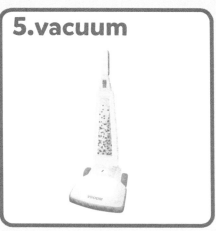

6.bucket

7.cleaner

8.duster

9.paper towel

1.vassoura	2.pá	3.esfregona
4.esponja	5.aspirador	6.balde
7.produto de limpeza	8.espanador	9.papel de cozinha

Home • Clean

1. to spray

2. to wipe
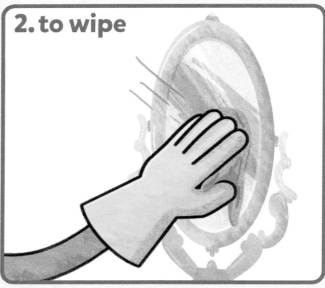

3. to sweep

4. to scrub

5. to clean

1. pulverizar

2. limpar

3. varrer

4. esfregar

5. limpar

Chapter 3
Clothes

Capítulo 3
Roupas

Clothes

1. shirt	2. pants	3. shorts

4. underwear	5. sock	6. shoes

7. sweater	8. jacket	9. hat

1. camisa	2. calças	3. calções
4. roupa interior	5. meia	6. sapatos
7. camisola	8. casaco	9. chapéu

Clothes

1. sandals

2. boots

3. sneakers

4. heel

5. sole

6. shoelace

7. to tie

8. to put on

9. to take off

1. sandálias	2. botas	3. ténis
4. salto alto	5. sola	6. atacador
7. atar	8. pôr	9. tirar

Clothes · Girls

1. dress

2. skirt
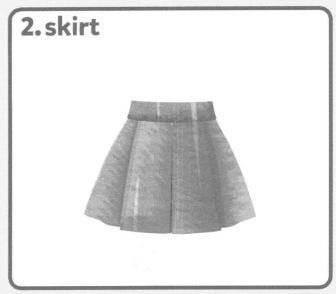

3. bikini

4. make-up

5. purse
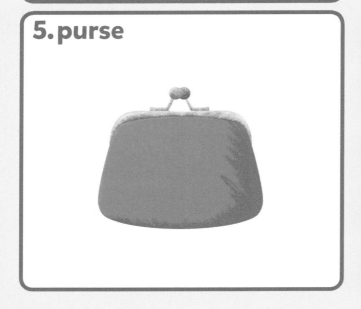

1. vestido

2. saia

3. bikini

4. maquilhagem

5. bolsa

Roupas · Raparigas

Clothes • Boys

1. jeans

2. t-shirt

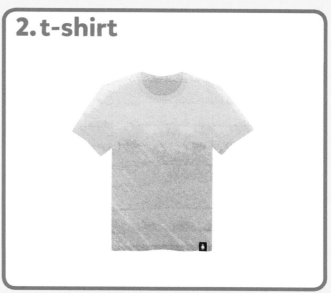

3. baseball cap

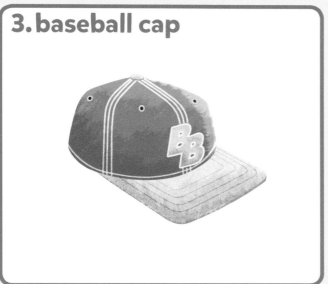

4. swimming trunks

1. calças de ganga

2. camiseta

3. boné de baseball

4. calções de banho

5. carteira

5. wallet

Clothes • Accessories

1. belt

2. scarf

3. watch

4. ring

5. necklace

6. earring

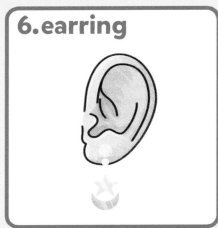

7. bracelet

8. cowboy hat

9. glove

1. cinto	2. cachecol	3. relógio
4. anel	5. colar	6. brinco
7. pulseira	8. chapéu de cowboy	9. luva

Roupas • Acessórios

Clothes - Accessories

1. pocket 	**2. sleeve** 	**3. collar** 
4. hood 	**5. zipper** 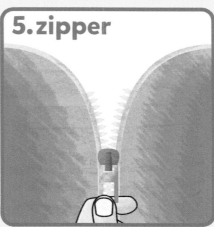	**6. button** 
7. buckle 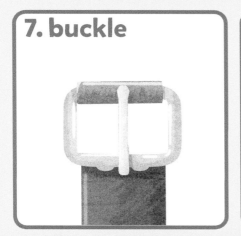	**8. patch** 	**9. logo** 

1. bolso	2. manga	3. colarinho
4. capuz	5. fecho	6. botão
7. fivela	8. remendo	9. logotipo

Clothes · Style

1. solid 	**2. striped** 	**3. polka dot** 
4. small 	**5. medium** 	**6. torn** 
7. large 	**8. extra-large** 	**9. stained** 

1. sólido	2. listado	3. bolinhas
4. pequeno	5. médio	6. rasgado
7. grande	8. extra grande	9. manchado

Roupas · Estilo

Clothes • Style

1. new

2. used

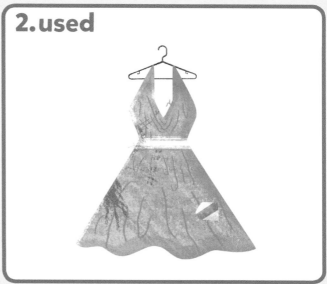

3. tight

4. loose

1. novo

2. usado

3. apertado

4. folgado

5. estilo

5. style

Clothes · Laundry

1. washer

2. dryer

3. detergent

4. basket

5. laundry

6. hanger

7. iron

8. wrinkle

9. crease

1. máquina de lavar 2. máquina de secar 3. detergente

4. cesto 5. roupa suja 6. cabide

7. ferro de engomar 8. ruga 9. vinco

Roupas · Lavandaria

Clothes · Laundry

1. to try

2. to wear

3. to fold
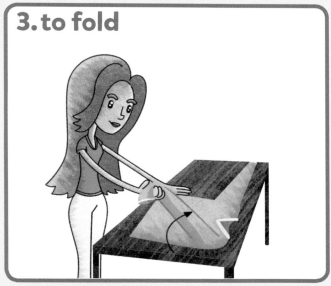

4. to put

1. tentar

2. vestir

3. dobrar

4. pôr

5. pendurar

5. to hang

Clothes

1. uniform

2. costume

3. pajamas

4. suit

5. robe

1. uniforme

2. traje

3. pijama

4. fato

5. robe

Chapter 4
Food

Capítulo 4
Comida

Food

1. fruit

2. vegetable

3. meat

4. bread

5. condiment

1. fruta

2. vegetal

3. carne

4. pão

5. condimento

Food

1. breakfast

2. lunch

3. dinner

4. beverage

5. dessert

1. pequeno-almoço

2. almoço

3. jantar

4. bebida

5. sobremesa

Food • Fruit

1. apple

2. banana

3. grapes

4. pineapple

5. strawberry

6. watermelon
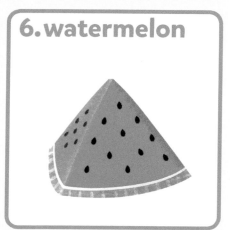

7. pumpkin

8. avocado

9. blueberry

1. maçã	2. banana	3. uvas
4. abacaxi	5. morango	6. melancia
7. abóbora	8. abacate	9. mirtilo

Comida • Fruta

Food · Fruit

1. raisin

2. orange

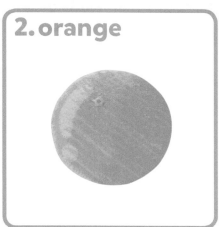

3. mango

4. coconut

5. lemon

6. lime

7. cherry

8. juicy

9. sour

1. passa	2. laranja	3. manga
4. côco	5. limão	6. lima
7. cereja	8. suculento	9. azedo

Comida · Fruta

Food · Vegetable

1. lettuce

2. celery

3. carrot

4. tomato

5. onion

6. cucumber

7. mushroom

8. broccoli

9. pickle

1. alface	2. aipo	3. cenoura
4. tomate	5. cebola	6. pepino
7. cogumelo	8. bróculo	9. pickle

Comida · Vegetais

Food · Vegetable

1. asparagus	2. corn	3. potato

4. chili pepper	5. garlic	6. peas

7. rotten	8. ripe	9. fresh

1. espargos	2. milho	3. batata
4. pimenta	5. alho	6. ervilhas
7. podre	8. maduro	9. fresco

Comida · Vegetais

Food • Breakfast

1. egg

2. bacon
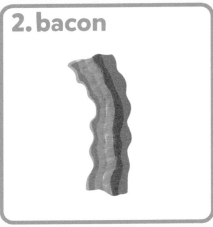

3. sausage

4. ham

5. pancakes

6. toast

7. cereal

8. butter

9. syrup

1. ovo	2. bacon	3. salsicha
4. fiambre	5. panquecas	6. torrada
7. cereal	8. manteiga	9. xarope

Comida • Pequeno-almoço

Food · Lunch

1. hamburger

2. fries

3. hotdog

4. chicken nugget
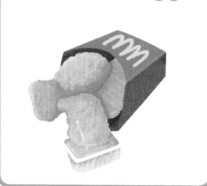

5. pizza
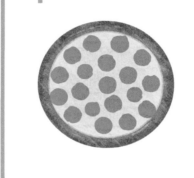

6. fish stick

7. sandwich

8. peanut butter

9. jelly

1. hamburguer
2. batatas fritas
3. cachorro-quente
4. nugget de frango
5. pizza
6. palito de peixe
7. sanduíche
8. manteiga de amendoim
9. geleia

Comida · Almoço

Food · Lunch

1. ketchup

2. mustard

3. mayonnaise

4. salt

5. cheese

6. lunch box

7. snack

8. spicy

9. sweet

1. ketchup	2. mostarda	3. maionese
4. sal	5. queijo	6. lancheira
7. lanche	8. picante	9. doce

Comida · Almoço

Food · Dinner

1. steak	2. chicken	3. pasta

4. soup	5. salad	6. salad dressing

7. beans	8. rice	9. sushi

1. bife	2. frango	3. massa
4. sopa	5. salada	6. tempero de salada
7. feijões	8. arroz	9. sushi

Comida · Jantar

Food · Dessert

1. candy	2. chips	3. cookie

4. donut	5. pie	6. cupcake

7. frosting	8. ice cream	9. chocolate

1. doce	2. batatas fritas	3. bolacha
4. donut	5. torta	6. cupcake
7. glacé	8. gelado	9. chocolate

Comida · Sobremesa

Food • Beverage

1. juice

2. milk

3. soda

4. tea

5. coffee

6. water

7. ice

8. empty

9. full

1. sumo	2. leite	3. refrigerante
4. chá	5. café	6. água
7. gelo	8. vazio	9. cheio

Comida • Bebida

Food • Cook

1. pan

2. pot

3. colander

4. spatula

5. tongs

6. ladle
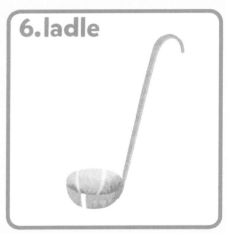

7. to prepare

8. to cook

9. to wash

1. frigideira	2. panela	3. escorredor
4. espátula	5. pinças	6. concha
7. preparar	8. cozinhar	9. lavar

Comida • Cozinhar

Food · Cook

1. to grill

2. to peel

3. to stir

4. to boil

5. to fry

6. to bake

7. to mix

8. to sprinkle

9. to heat

1. grelhar	2. descascar	3. mexer
4. ferver	5. fritar	6. cozer
7. misturar	8. polvilhar	9. aquecer

Comida · Cozinhar

Food · Eat

1. to eat

2. to drink

3. to chew

4. to burp

5. to pour

6. to dip

7. hungry

8. thirsty

9. delicious

1. comer	2. beber	3. mastigar
4. arrotar	5. verter	6. mergulhar
7. esfomeado	8. sedento	9. delicioso

Comida · Comer

Chapter 5
Health

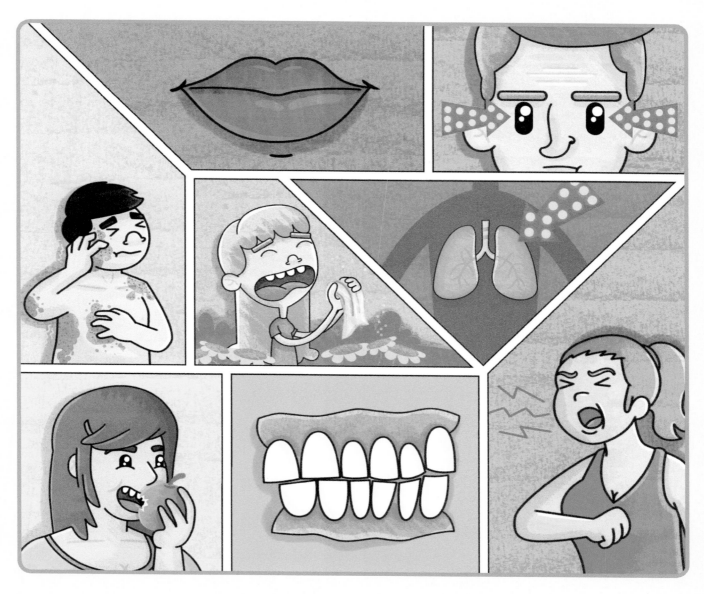

Capítulo 5
Saúde

Health

1. head

2. body

3. sick

4. hurt

5. healthy

1. cabeça

2. corpo

3. doente

4. magoado

5. saudável

Saúde

Health

1. brain
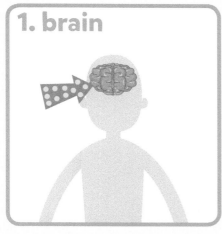

2. lungs
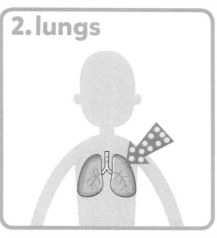

3. heart

4. blood
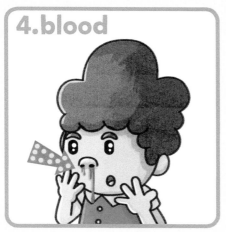

5. skin

6. muscle

7. bone

8. skull

9. skeleton

1. cérebro	2. pulmões	3. coração
4. sangue	5. pele	6. músculo
7. osso	8. crânio	9. esqueleto

Health • Head

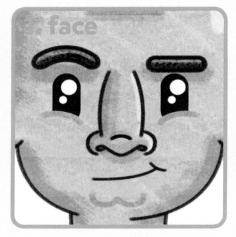
1. face

2. eye

3. nose

4. forehead

5. eyebrow

6. ear

7. cheek

8. chin

9. hair

1. cara	2. olho	3. nariz
4. testa	5. sobrancelha	6. orelha
7. bochecha	8. queixo	9. cabelo

Health • Head

1. mouth

2. lips

3. teeth
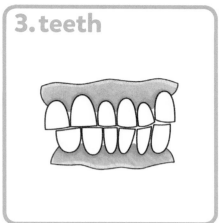

4. tongue
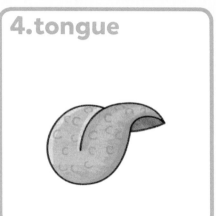

5. neck

6. to talk

7. to smile

8. to bite

9. to lick

1. boca	2. lábios	3. dentes
4. língua	5. pescoço	6. falar
7. sorrir	8. morder	9. lamber

Health • Body

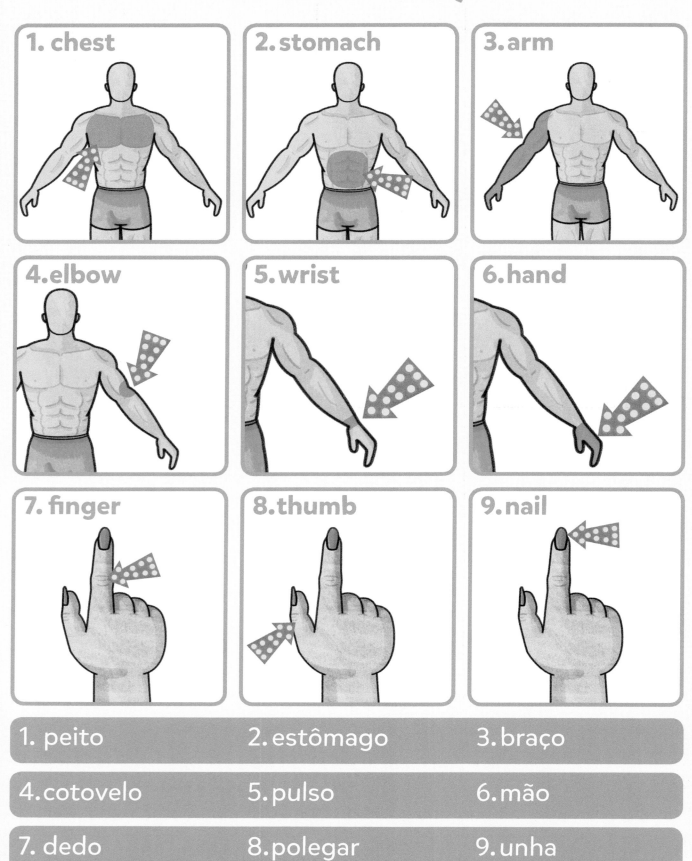

1. chest

2. stomach

3. arm

4. elbow

5. wrist

6. hand

7. finger

8. thumb

9. nail

1. peito	2. estômago	3. braço
4. cotovelo	5. pulso	6. mão
7. dedo	8. polegar	9. unha

Saúde • Corpo

Health • Body

1. back
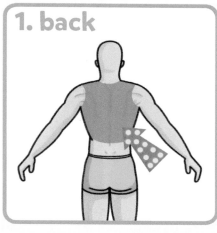

2. shoulder
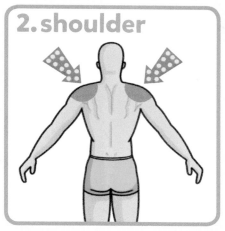

3. waist
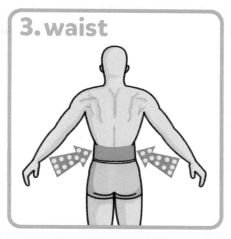

4. hips
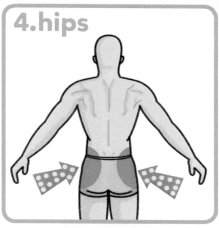

5. leg
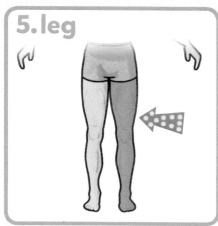

6. knee
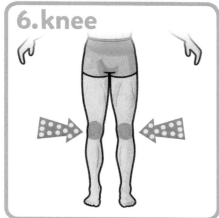

7. ankle
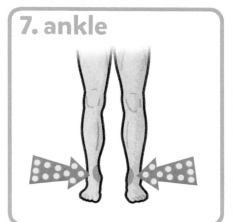

8. foot
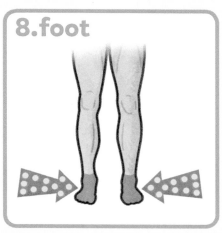

9. toe

1. costas	2. ombro	3. cintura
4. ancas	5. perna	6. joelho
7. tornozelo	8. pé	9. dedo do pé

Health • Sick

1. cold

2. fever
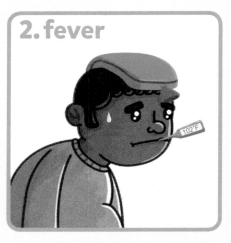

3. flu

4. headache

5. allergy

6. stomach ache

7. to cough

8. to sneeze

9. to vomit

1. frio	2. febre	3. gripe
4. dor de cabeça	5. alergia	6. dor de estômago
7. tossir	8. espirrar	9. vomitar

Saúde • Doente

Health · Hurt

1. cut

2. bruise

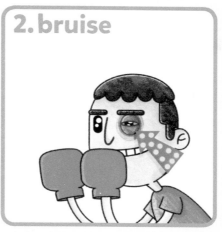

3. burn

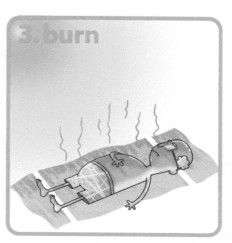

4. rash

5. bite

6. pain

7. swollen (*finger*)

8. broken (*bone*)

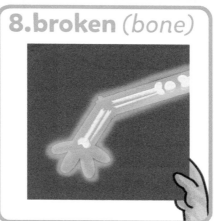

9. to bleed

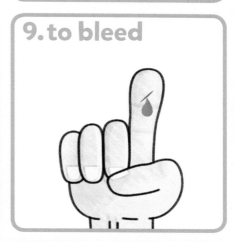

1. corte	2. nódoa negra	3. queimadura
4. erupção cutânea	5. mordida	6. dor
7. inchado	8. partido	9. sangrar

Health • Healthy

1. to see

2. to hear

3. to taste

4. to smell

5. to touch

6. to breathe

7. to sweat

8. strong

9. weak

1. ver	2. ouvir	3. provar
4. cheirar	5. tocar	6. respirar
7. suar	8. forte	9. fraco

Chapter 6
School

Capítulo 6
Escola

School

1. office

2. classroom

3. cafeteria

4. field

5. auditorium

6. gym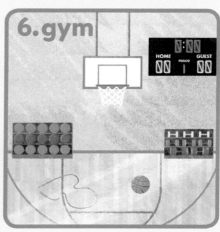

7. playground

8. restroom

9. hallway

1. escritório	2. sala de aula	3. refeitório
4. campo	5. auditório	6. ginásio
7. recreio	8. casa de banho	9. corredor

Escola

School

1. principal

2. teacher

3. student

4. janitor

5. nurse

6. classmate

7. guard

8. fountain

9. locker

1. diretor	2. professor	3. estudante
4. contínuo	5. enfermeiro	6. colega de aula
7. guarda escolar	8. bebedouro	9. cacifo

School · Classroom

1. whiteboard

2. marker

3. desk

4. projector

5. screen

6. chair

7. clock

8. waste basket

9. flag

1. quadro branco	2. marcador	3. carteira escolar
4. projetor	5. ecrã	6. cadeira
7. relógio	8. cesto de lixo	9. bandeira

School · Classroom

1. to teach

2. to learn

3. to study

4. to think

1. ensinar

2. aprender

3. estudar

4. pensar

5. graduar

5. to graduate

School • Math

1. math	2. odd	3. even
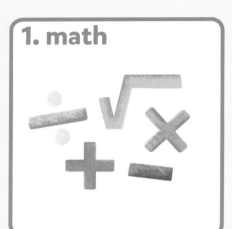		

4. calculator	5. to add	6. to subtract
	$2 + 2 = 4$	$3 - 1 = 2$

7. to multiply	8. to divide	9. to equal
$5 \times 2 = 10$	$8 \div 4 = 2$	

1. matemática	2. ímpar	3. par
4. calculadora	5. adicionar	6. subtrair
7. multiplicar	8. dividir	9. igualar

School • Science

1. science

2. experiment

3. scientist

4. microscope
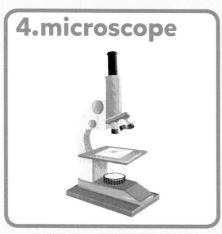

5. atom
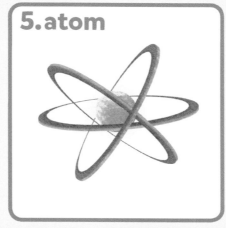

6. cell
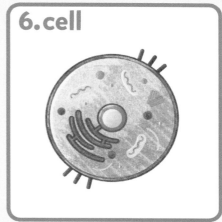

7. robot

8. electricity

9. magnet

1. ciência	2. experiência	3. cientista
4. microscópio	5. átomo	6. célula
7. robot	8. electricidade	9. íman

School · English

1. language

2. alphabet

3. letter

4. word

5. sentence

6. dictionary

7. to listen

8. to read

9. to write

1. idioma	2. alfabeto	3. letra
4. palavra	5. frase	6. dicionário
7. ouvir	8. ler	9. escrever

School · Lesson

1. lesson

2. homework

3. test

4. question
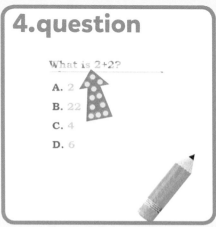

5. easy

6. difficult

7. answer

8. to remember

9. to forget

1. aula	2. tarefa escolar	3. teste
4. pergunta	5. fácil	6. difícil
7. resposta	8. lembrar	9. esquecer

Escola · Aula

School · Supplies

1. pencil

2. pen

3. crayon

4. backpack

5. paper

6. eraser

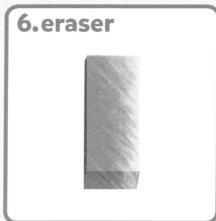

7. scissors

8. glue

9. ruler

1. lápis	2. caneta	3. lápis de cera
4. mochila	5. papel	6. apagador
7. tesoura	8. cola	9. régua

Escola · Materiais

School • Supplies

1. to color

2. to glue

3. to erase

4. to cut
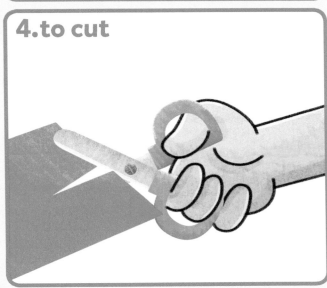

1. colorir

2. colar

3. apagar

4. cortar

5. medir

5. to measure
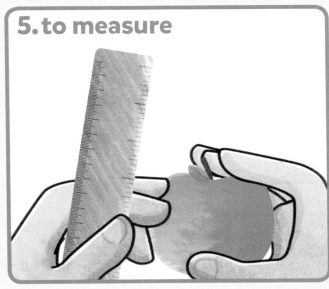

School · Computer

1. computer

2. laptop

3. mouse

4. monitor

5. keyboard

6. printer

7. speaker

8. to type

9. to select

1. computador	2. portátil	3. rato
4. monitor	5. teclado	6. impressora
7. altifalante	8. digitar	9. selecionar

Escola · Computador

School • Internet

1. internet

2. website

3. to search

4. username

5. password

6. to log in

7. email

8. to send

9. to download

1. internet	2. website	3. procurar
4. nome de utilizador	5. palavra passe	6. entrar
7. email	8. enviar	9. baixar

School

1. elementary
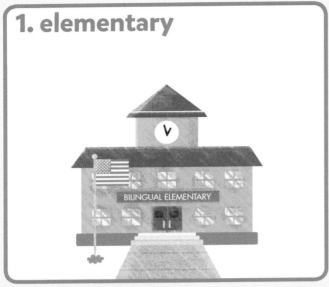

2. middle school
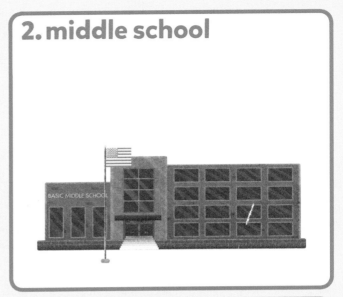

3. high school
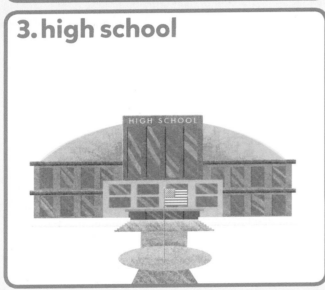

4. college
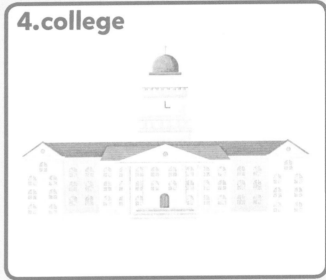

5. school bus

1. primária

2. básico

3. secundária

4. faculdade

5. autocarro escolar

Chapter 7
City

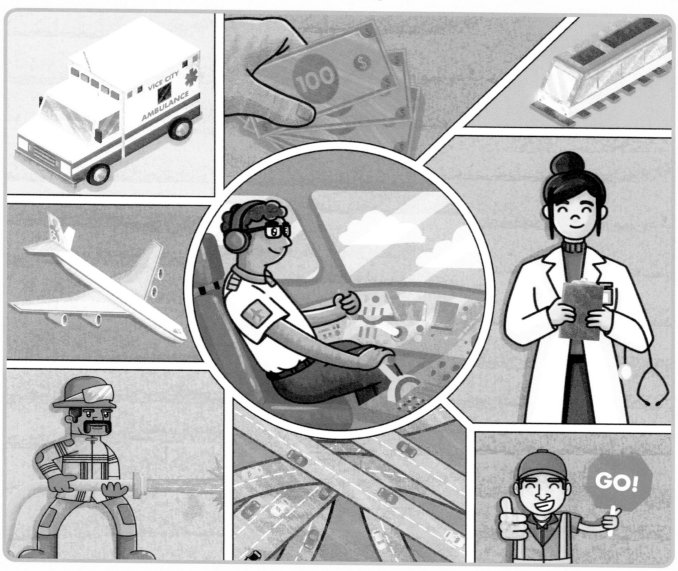

Capítulo 7
Cidade

City

1. city
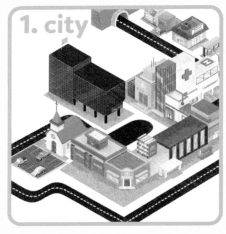

2. church

3. post office

4. police station

5. fire station

6. city hall

7. airport

8. hospital

9. library

1. cidade	2. igreja	3. correios
4. esquadra da polícia	5. quartel dos bombeiros	6. câmara municipal
7. aeroporto	8. hospital	9. biblioteca

City

1. bank

2. museum

3. court house

4. auto shop

5. gas station

6. bus stop

7. parking lot

8. bridge

9. tunnel

1. banco   2. museu   3. tribunal

4. loja de carros   5. posto de gasolina   6. autocarro

7. estacionamento   8. ponte   9. túnel

Cidade

City • Car

1. car

2. truck

3. motorcycle

4. semi-truck

5. garbage truck

6. taxi

7. bus

8. train

9. subway
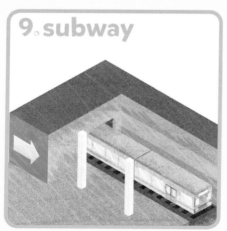

1. carro	2. camioneta	3. mota
4. camião	5. camião do lixo	6. táxi
7. autocarro	8. comboio	9. metro

Cidade • Carro

City • Car

1. headlight

2. windshield

3. bumper

4. hood

5. license plate

6. tire

7. engine

8. steering wheel

9. gas

1. farol	2. para-brisas	3. para-choques
4. capô	5. matrícula	6. pneu
7. motor	8. volante	9. gasolina

City • Traffic

1. traffic

2. traffic light

3. sign

4. intersection
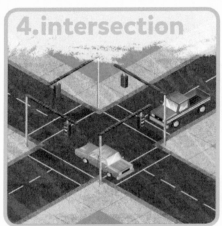

5. corner

6. sidewalk

7. crosswalk

8. street

9. highway

1. trânsito	2. semáforo	3. sinal
4. intersecção	5. esquina	6. calçada
7. passadeira	8. rua	9. autoestrada

City • Traffic

1. to go	2. to stop	3. to cross

4. to get on	5. to get off	6. to wait

7. to drive	8. to park	9. to crash

1. ir	2. parar	3. atravessar
4. entrar	5. sair	6. esperar
7. conduzir	8. estacionar	9. colidir

City · Library

1. librarian

2. book

3. magazine

4. newspaper

5. map

6. title

7. to look

8. to get

9. to return

1. bibliotecário	2. livro	3. revista
4. jornal	5. mapa	6. título
7. procurar	8. obter	9. devolver

City • Hospital

1. doctor

2. patient
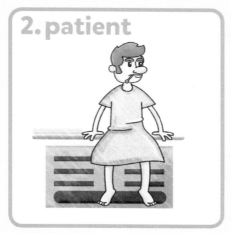

3. ambulance
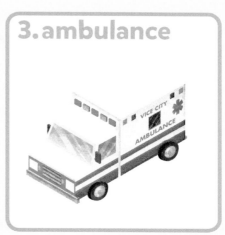

4. medicine

5. crutch

6. wheelchair

7. injection
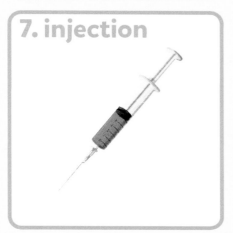

8. cast
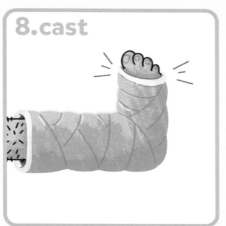

9. X-ray

1. médico	2. paciente	3. ambulância
4. medicamento	5. muleta	6. cadeira de rodas
7. injecção	8. gesso	9. raio-x

City • Bank

1. teller

2. money

3. coin

4. check
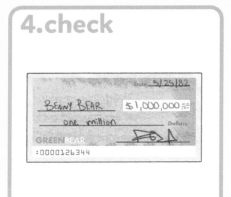

5. debit card

6. PIN number

7. to deposit

8. to withdraw

9. to save

1. caixa	2. dinheiro	3. moeda
4. cheque	5. cartão de débito	6. número pin
7. depositar	8. retirar	9. poupar

Cidade • Banco

City · Safety

1. police car	2. crime	3. police officer

4. fire truck	5. fire	6. fire fighter

7. airplane	8. passenger	9. pilot

1. carro da polícia   2. crime   3. polícia

4. camião dos bombeiros   5. fogo   6. bombeiro

7. avião   8. passageiro   9. piloto

City • Jobs

1. trash collector

2. judge

3. mayor

4. mail carrier

5. driver

6. engineer

7. security

8. architect

9. lawyer

1. lixeiro	2. juíz	3. presidente da câmara
4. carteiro	5. condutor	6. engenheiro
7. segurança	8. arquiteto	9. advogado

Chapter 8
Life

Capítulo 8
Vida

Life • Good

1. good

2. quiet

3. smart

4. confident

5. to work

1. bom

2. sossegado

3. inteligente

4. confiante

5. trabalhar

Vida • Bom

Life • Bad

2. noisy

3. lazy

4. nervous

1. mau

2. barulhento

3. preguiçoso

4. nervoso

5. roubar

5. to steal

Life • Store

1. mall

2. store

3. groceries

4. cart

5. line

6. register

7. expensive
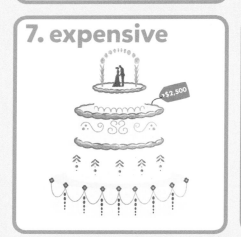

8. cheap

9. to buy

1. centro comercial	2. loja	3. compras
4. carrinho de compras	5. fila	6. caixa registadora
7. caro	8. barato	9. comprar

Vida • Loja

Life • Restaurant

1. chef

2. waiter

3. customer

4. straw
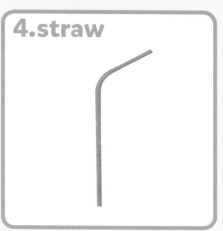

5. lid

6. menu

7. drive-through

8. to order

9. to ask

1. chef	2. empregado de mesa	3. cliente
4. palhinha	5. tampa	6. menu
7. drive-through	8. pedir	9. perguntar

Vida • Restaurante

Life • Phone

1. cell phone

2. to call

3. message

4. camera

5. picture

6. battery

7. to record

8. video

Cat sings the national anthem!!!! WOW!
1,230,930 views

9. to charge

1. telemóvel	2. ligar	3. mensagem
4. câmera	5. imagem	6. bateria
7. gravar	8. vídeo	9. carregar

Life · Music

1. guitar

2. drums

3. piano

4. violin

5. flute
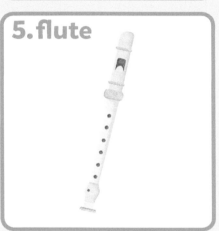

6. trumpet

7. band

8. concert

9. to sing

1. guitarra	2. bateria	3. piano
4. violino	5. flauta	6. trombeta
7. banda	8. concerto	9. cantar

1. movie

2. show

3. cartoon

4. park

5. bowling

6. arcade

7. zoo

8. roller coaster
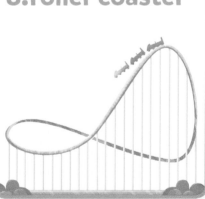

9. to ride

1. filme	2. programa de televisão	3. desenhos animados
4. parque	5. bowling	6. arcada
7. jardim zoológico	8. montanha russa	9. andar

Life • Park

1. swing 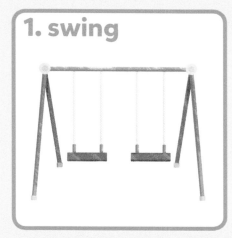	**2. slide** 	**3. monkey bars** 
4. bench 	**5. to run** 	**6. to climb** 
7. to push 	**8. to pull** 	**9. to like** 

1. baloiço	2. escorrega	3. barras de macaco
4. banco	5. correr	6. escalar
7. empurrar	8. puxar	9. gostar

Vida • Parque

Life • Sports

1. baseball

2. volleyball

3. basketball

4. football

5. soccer

6. hockey

7. tennis

8. golf

9. cricket

1. basebol	2. voleibol	3. basquetebol
4. futebol americano	5. futebol	6. hóquei
7. ténis	8. golfe	9. críquete

Life · Sports

1. surfing

2. snowboarding

3. skating

4. boxing

5. wrestling

6. gymnastics

7. ring

8. stadium

9. track
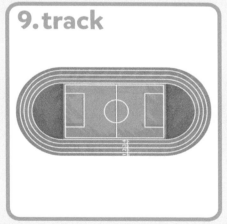

1. surfar	2. snowboard	3. skate
4. boxe	5. luta	6. ginástica
7. ringue	8. estádio	9. pista

Life • Sports

1. uniform

2. helmet

3. cleats

4. bat

5. goal

6. net
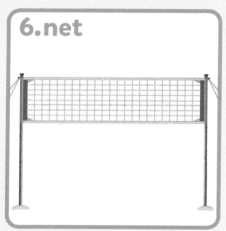

7. to stretch

8. to exercise

9. to practice

1. uniforme

2. capacete

3. chuteiras

4. taco de basebol

5. baliza

6. rede

7. esticar

8. exercitar

9. praticar

Life · Sports

1. to win

2. to lose

3. to score

4. to throw

5. to catch

6. to kick

7. to jump

8. to race

9. to hit

1. ganhar	2. perder	3. pontuar
4. atirar	5. apanhar	6. chutar
7. saltar	8. fazer uma corrida	9. bater

1. athlete

2. team

3. coach

4. referee

5. fan

1. atleta

2. equipa

3. treinador

4. árbitro

5. adepto

Chapter 9
Nature

Nature · Plants

1. tree

2. bush

3. plant

4. branch

5. leaf

6. root

7. trunk

8. shade

9. to grow

1. árvore	2. arbusto	3. planta
4. ramo	5. folha	6. raíz
7. tronco	8. sombra	9. crescer

Natureza · Plantas

Nature • Plants

1. cactus

2. palm tree

3. pine tree

4. flower

5. thorn

6. stem
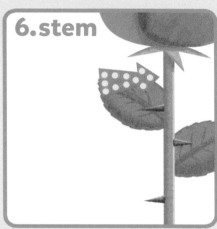

7. seed

8. soil

9. pot

1. cacto	2. palmeira	3. pinheiro
4. flor	5. espinho	6. caule
7. semente	8. terra	9. vaso de plantas

Nature • Earth

1. Earth

2. land

3. mountain

4. desert

5. jungle

6. forest

7. island

8. hill

9. valley

1. Terra	2. terra	3. montanha
4. deserto	5. selva	6. floresta
7. ilha	8. colina	9. vale

Natureza • Terra

Nature · Earth

1. ocean

2. river

3. lake

4. waterfall

5. beach

6. wave
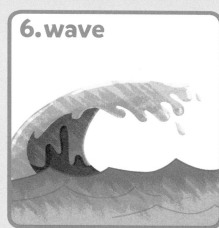

7. mud

8. sand

9. rock

1. oceano	2. rio	3. lago
4. cascata	5. praia	6. onda
7. lama	8. areia	9. rocha

Natureza · Terra

Nature · Space

1. planet

2. stars

3. comet

4. sun

5. moon

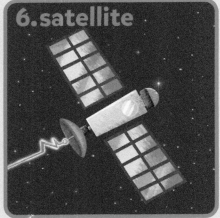
6. satellite

7. astronaut

8. alien

9. to explore

1. planeta	2. estrelas	3. cometa
4. sol	5. lua	6. satélite
7. astronauta	8. alienígena	9. explorar

Natureza · Espaço

Nature • Weather

1. day

2. night

3. morning

4. spring

5. summer

6. afternoon

7. fall

8. winter

1. dia	2. noite	3. manhã
4. primavera	5. verão	6. tarde
7. outono	8. inverno	9. fim de tarde

Natureza • Clima

Nature • Weather

1. rain

2. lightning

3. storm

4. sky

5. cloud

6. snow

7. fog

8. puddle

9. umbrella

1. chuva	2. relâmpago	3. tempestade
4. céu	5. nuvem	6. neve
7. nevoeiro	8. poça	9. guarda-chuva

Natureza • Clima

Nature • Weather

1. hot

2. warm

3. cold

4. temperature

5. to melt

6. to freeze

7. sunny

8. cloudy

9. windy

1. quente	2. morno	3. frio
4. temperatura	5. derreter	6. congelar
7. ensolarado	8. nublado	9. ventoso

Nature • Environment

1. tornado

2. volcano

3. tidal wave

4. hurricane

5. flood

6. avalanche

7. wildfire

8. drought

9. earthquake

1. tornado	2. vulcão	3. maremoto
4. furacão	5. inundação	6. avalanche
7. incêndio florestal	8. seca	9. terramoto

Natureza • Meio Ambiente

Nature • Environment

1. to help

2. to rescue

3. to take

4. to give

1. ajudar

2. resgatar

3. tirar

4. dar

5. partilhar

5. to share

Nature • Environment

1. to recycle

2. to litter

3. to use

4. to waste

5. pollution

1. reciclar

2. fazer lixo

3. usar

4. desperdiçar

5. poluição

Natureza • Meio Ambiente

Chapter 10
Animals

Capítulo 10
Animais

Animals · Farm

1. cow

2. pig

3. chicken

4. donkey

5. horse

6. turkey

7. goat

8. sheep

9. farm

1. vaca	2. porco	3. frango
4. burro	5. cavalo	6. perú
7. cabra	8. ovelha	9. quinta

Animals • Ocean

1. fish

2. shark

3. squid

4. octopus

5. crab

6. whale

7. dolphin

8. seal

9. to swim

1. peixe	2. tubarão	3. lula
4. polvo	5. caranguejo	6. baleia
7. golfinho	8. foca	9. nadar

Animals • Forest

1. bear

2. raccoon

3. porcupine

4. deer

5. skunk

6. wolf

7. fur

8. cave

9. to howl

1. urso	2. guaxinim	3. porco-espinho
4. veado	5. doninha	6. lobo
7. pêlo	8. caverna	9. uivar

Animals • Jungle

1. panda

2. lion

3. crocodile

4. monkey

5. elephant

6. snake

7. giraffe

8. zebra

9. camel

1. panda	2. leão	3. crocodilo
4. macaco	5. elefante	6. cobra
7. girafa	8. zebra	9. camelo

Animals · Birds

1. bird

2. wing

3. beak

4. feather

5. claw

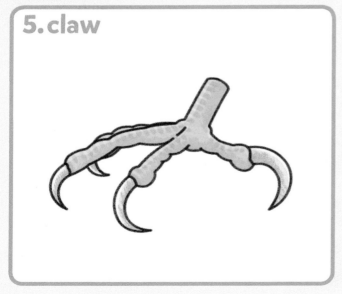

1. pássaro

2. asa

3. bico

4. pena

5. garra

Animals • Birds

1. eagle

2. owl

3. duck

4. penguin

5. peacock

6. hummingbird

7. flamingo

8. nest

9. to fly

1. águia	2. coruja	3. pato
4. pinguim	5. pavão	6. beija-flor
7. flamingo	8. ninho	9. voar

Animals • Pets

1. dog

2. puppy

3. lizard

4. cat

5. kitten

6. frog

7. rabbit

8. goldfish
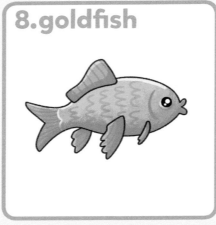

9. turtle

1. cão	2. cachorro	3. lagarto
4. gato	5. gatinho	6. rã
7. coelho	8. peixe-dourado	9. tartaruga

Animals • Pets

1. leash

2. collar
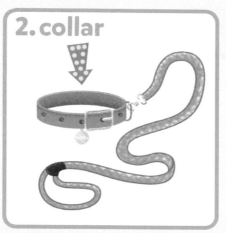

3. aquarium

4. cage

5. to feed

6. to pet

7. to chase

8. to train

9. to walk

1. trela	2. coleira	3. aquário
4. jaula	5. alimentar	6. dar uma festa
7. perseguir	8. treinar	9. passear o cão

Animals · Insects

1. bee

2. mosquito
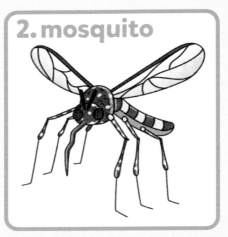

3. fly

4. butterfly

5. spider
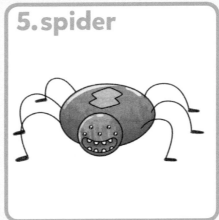

6. web

7. ant

8. snail

9. shell

1. abelha	2. mosquito	3. mosca
4. borboleta	5. aranha	6. teia
7. formiga	8. caracol	9. concha

Animais · Insetos

Glossary

Glossary

C

Glossary

Glossary

E

F

Glossary

Glossary

Glossary

Glossary

Glossary

Q

R

S

Glossary

Glossary

T

Glossary

Glossary

X